Pens
FROM THE WOOD LATHE

Dick Sing

STEP-BY-STEP INSTRUCTIONS FOR THE WOOD TURNER

Schiffer Publishing Ltd®

Dedication

This goes out to all my wood turning friends, mentors, and suppliers whose contributions have helped bring me this far. Most especially to my "inherited son" Rex Burningham, a young, gifted friend who is a fine turner from Utah.

Gallery set-up by Cindy Sing.

Library of Congress Cataloging-in-Publication Data
Sing, Dick.
Pens from the wood lathe/Dick Sing.
p. cm.
ISBN 0-88740-939-3 (paper)
1. Turning. 2. Lathes. 3. Pens. 4. Pencils. I. Title.
TT201.S46 1996
674'.88--dc20   95-37217 CIP

ISBN: 0-88740-939-3
Printed in China

This book is meant only for personal home use and recreation. It is not intended for commercial applications or manufacturing purposes.

Published by Schiffer Publishing Ltd.
4880 Lower Valley Road
Atglen, PA 19310
Phone: (610) 593-1777; Fax: (610) 593-2002
E-mail: Schifferbk@aol.com
Please visit our web site catalog at
www.schifferbooks.com

This book may be purchased from the publisher.
Include $3.95 for shipping.
Please try your bookstore first.
We are always looking for authors to write books on new and related subjects. If you have an idea for a book please contact us at the address above.
You may write for a free printed catalog.

In Europe, Schiffer books are distributed by
Bushwood Books
6 Marksbury Avenue
Kew Gardens
Surrey TW9 4JF England
Phone: 44 (0)208-392-8585; Fax: 44 (0)208-392-9876
E-mail: Bushwd@aol.com
Free postage in the U.K., Europe; air mail at cost.

Contents

Acknowledgments

Thanks to the following companies who provided equipment, materials and encouragement for this book: The Berea Hardwood Co., Berea, Ohio; Bonham's Woodworking Supply, Inc., Garland, Texas; Craft Supplies, U.S.A., Provo, Utah; Packard Woodworks, Tryon, North Carolina; Hut Products, Sturgeon, Missouri; One Good Turn, Murray, Utah; Woodcuts Ltd., Racine, Wisconsin; and Woodcraft Supply Corporation, Parkersburg, West Virginia.

Purpose

The purpose of this book is to show people how to construct a quality writing instrument from wood, and I do mean quality. Whatever we do, we want to do it with pride and our best workmanship. We don't just want to make a pen. Precision will pay off with a pen or pencil that looks good, feels good, and works well.

These pens and pencils are so beautiful that they will become keepers--family treasures, heirlooms. People keep track of them so they don't lose them.

As a gift, they are one of a kind--your friend will not have received one just like it in his stocking. For the same reasons, these writing instruments are excellent sellers at craft and art shows. They do not look like high school shop projects, although they could be.

As a woodturner, I bet you can't make just one. Because they are fun to make, they are habit forming. The more pens you turn, the more you want to improve on materials and quality.

Some History

When man first started "writing" he used burnt stick ends--nothing more than charcoal quills. He progressed to metal tips, and inkwells in the desk and then to fountain pens, cartridge fountain pens, graphite pencils, and mechanical pencils. Most people my age grew up with #2 pencils made by either Farber or Dixon. We longed to own one of those sharp mechanical pencils that you didn't have to sharpen. We were attracted by the mystery of the magical lead that appeared at the twist of the fingers.

Then pen technology moved to ballpoint pens, clickers, twisters and the ones with the button to push, felt tip pens, rollerball, and pressurized ball points that can be used in the weightlessness of space. Here, finally, we have returned to the handcrafted beauty and comfort of the wooden pen. Since I love wood, I thank the people who brought back the demand for wooden pens and pencils. This movement to handcrafted pens started with wood and has progressed to beautiful man-made materials like Dymondwood, Colorwood, Corian®, Decora, crushed velvet, celluloid acetate and impregnated woods.

Blank Selection

Our choice of wood or material determines what our pens will look like. In my opinion, plastic is cold--wood is warm, and adheres to ones hand, as one living being to another. Wood reeks of life & has a multitude of colors patterns, textures, and emotional attachments For me, it's life, it's my favorite material, it's wood.

Many people prefer the man-made materials, again for their colors, textures, and uniqueness. Each material has its own qualities which affect durability, how it turns, and how it finishes. Different special effects are possible, depending on the combination of materials used and how we handle them.

Selecting wood for a pen blank can be different than selecting wood for a larger piece. Some people think that a board with an attractive grain will make an outstanding pen which is not necessarily true. In board form the grain may be very attractive, but when we reduce it down to the size of a pen, very little of what made the board appealing remains.

This piece of oak is cut through the crotch area. As you can see, the grain is much tighter, pores are almost non-existent. The variations in color make a nice pattern on the pen diameter and the iridescent qualities, which are much more pronounced on this one, make it an outstanding selection for a pen.

As you can see, the wood block shows a good solid grain for furniture or other large projects. The turned blank, on the other hand, has lost all the desirable features. Very blasé.

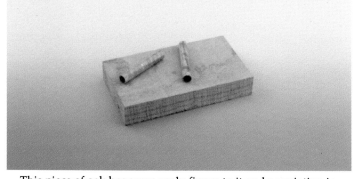

This piece of oak has some curly figure to it and a variation in color. The pores are much different than those in the first sample. This is a much better selection for making a pen, as the grain and pores will still show up when the block is reduced to the diameter of the pen.

Grain color and figure are not always apparent. Wetting the surface with your finger and good old spit will enable you to predict what the wood will look like with finish.

The effect of pores has a major impact on the final appearance. Vermillion (padauk), for example, has a beautiful reddish color, but has very large pores which darken as you finish them. Most of the time they never completely fill. One alternative wood which would provide a beautiful red color is bloodwood. The colors are very similar, but bloodwood has finer pores and will take a smoother finish.

Wood Color

Between the domestic and exotic woods, a wide range of colors are available, from red to yellow, to green, to a spectrum of colors in between, including black. Nature has been very generous with its palette.

Grain Patterns

Grain patterns can be classified into several different groups. Good choices for pens are:

·*Burl* with an eye pattern will be much more pronounced than a burl with a marbled pattern. On the other hand, the marbled pattern can have an array of colors which the eye pattern may not have.

·Some *fiddleback* has alternating rays that are much more distinctive in flash and depth. Some also have rays which are closer together, making a better choice for pens.

·*Crotch* figure always makes spectacular pens. This wood is created when two branches are knit together. In addition to the flashy grain patterns, the wood has the potential for spectacular color. It is not the easiest wood to turn, but the results are well worth the effort.

·*Birdseye* is another fine choice. Again select for the tightest knot pattern. The finished wood is a teaser. The iridescence around the eyes creates an impression of a very three dimensional surface. People expect the pen to feel somewhat rough, and yet it is difficult to find a smoother finish than birdseye maple. Other woods can provide a birdseye pattern, but these patterns are rare compared to the maple.

·*Spalted wood* is created by a fungus that is the forerunner of rot in dead trees. The fungus stains the wood, creating black lines that look as if they were drawn with a calligraphy pen. Spalting can also create varied colors. Sometimes the colors create mottled or speckled patterns. If we dry the wood and stop the spalting process while the wood is still solid, we can retain the exciting patterns. Timing is everything. With a premature harvest, you lose the spalting. If you wait too long, the wood rots.

Backyard Finds

Sometimes the most exciting discoveries are found by accident. Someone trims a large lilac bush, or an ornamental shrub yields a treasure. Redbud, sumac, honeysuckle, and yew can provide beautiful wood. Keep your mind and eyes open. Don't limit yourself to the woods that you have read about.

The firewood pile can yield a mother lode. We can find anything from spalding, blue stain, to mineral stain. Since the wood is exposed, you will see patterns and potential that will not be apparent in a standing tree. This is also an easy way to harvest a crop without a great deal of labor since the tree is already felled and stacked.

We are looking for anything out of the ordinary, anything distinctive, a one-of-a-kind treasure, as these will make our pens unique. No factory can compete with our relentless search and our exhilarating discovery of materials.

The Down Side

Now that we have discussed the beauty and fun of wood types, we must, in all honesty, consider some of the drawbacks associated with some of our choices. Some of our exotics, such as cocobolo and greenheart, to name just two of a long list, can cause an allergic reaction in some people. Spalted woods, formed by a fungus, also can cause reactions. The dust is usually the culprit because we breathe it. Dust collectors can't collect it all. Masks can't filter it all. Our main intention is to make people aware of the situation and treat it with caution.

Secondly, after praising all of our fancy and unique grains, they can provide extra challenges for drilling and turning. The very qualities which create beautiful variations, can deflect the drill bit. With varied grains, somewhere on the pen we are turning against the grain. It can be frustrating to have a one-of-a-kind piece chip, tear, or break your heart. And they do. First time turners would probably be better off to cut their turning teeth on easier woods before tackling the choice cuts. However, I know it's hard to eat hamburger when you know about steak.

Alternatives to Natural Wood

Dymondwood
Dymondwood is hardwood veneers, impregnated with resins and color dyes and bonded under high temperatures and pressure. The resulting material is very hard, uniform, and the finish is a part of the wood itself, requiring only buffing with compounds to bring out its luster. Solid colors and a variety of color combinations are available. Dymondwood can also be cut and reglued into a multitude of patterns. It can be brittle for turning and the layers sometimes have a tendency to lift which results in chipping. I feel the pluses outweigh the minuses.

Colorwood
Colorwood is very similar to Dymondwood, but it does not have the range of colors and is subject to fading from direct sunlight. It does provide some color choices which are not available in Dymondwood, especially in the pastel and pink ranges.

Corian®
Corian was developed as a countertop material. Similar products are available under a raft of different trade names. They are all basically the same, although some differences in consistency and color choices exist. Corian resembles stone and cannot be mistaken for wood. It is also more durable than wood, does not fade, and can be refinished by buffing. Compound and cloth wheels elicit a perfect finish. It can be drilled and cut with the same tools used for wood.

Decora, Crushed Velvet, or Celluloid Acetate
These materials were used in the 1920s for the world class elite pens. They can be marbled, translucent, or colorful, providing a striking appearance. They cut and drill easily, like butter. With cloth wheels and compound, they buff to a glass-like finish. Care needs to be used when sanding or working as they are easily scratched. Start with finer grits than normal when sanding. While this is not my favorite (I prefer the warmth of wood), in an art decor environment, this material can be extremely dramatic.

Impregnated woods
Any wood can be impregnated with resins which then permeate the entire piece. This treatment provides stability and water resistance to woods which are borderline, such as punky or spalting woods, or those that are too soft for workability. Dye can be introduced in the process as well. The results can create startling products. The finish is normally built in, like Dymondwood, so all that is necessary is to buff it. All woods are not equal. Some woods respond better to the treatment than others. It is also expensive.

Standard Twist Pen

Drilling Equipment

A drill press is the tool of choice, although if necessary drilling can be done carefully by hand or in the lathe. I prefer the drill press as it gives me a better feel of drilling. It is also faster, especially with multiple projects, since I can establish a positive set-up which allows me to drill uniform blocks without relocating each piece.

First let's create a positive set-up. To protect the drill table, lay down a wooden block of uniform thickness. On top of the block position a vee block and use a hand clamp to secure the set-up to the drill table.

Mark the center of your blank and, with a second hand clamp, clamp the blank in the vee block. Using a pointer or the tip of a brad point drill, locate the vee block set-up so the drill is centered to the work piece. This set-up allows you to drill just one blank or any number of blanks, as long as the blanks are all square and the same size.

When I cut my pen blanks, I try to make them square, an essential step in making the set-up work. I then cut my blank length into two sections. I make each blank section a little longer than the length of the brass tubes from the pen kit I will be using in case I have blow out (jagged hole after drilling). When I cut my blank apart, I mark a line with a felt tip pen on the center section of the same surface so I can always realign the grain accurately.

The drill has a tendency to wander or be deflected by the grain. If you drill both sections from the center, any variations in the alignment where the two parts meet will be minimal, increasing the ability to match the grains. Any error will show up more at the ends where it is less noticeable. To accomplish this, we must identify two common surfaces. I have marked two set-up sides, one in black, one in white, to make it easier to see what I am doing.

I have carried the tape over to the center ends (the ends where the grain alignment mark was drawn), so that you can see exactly how you will need to place the blank section in the vee block for drilling.

Set the blank in the vee so that the black and white surfaces touch the vee block and the center section is towards the drill. You will notice that on the left side of the exposed surfaces is our grain aligning mark.

To set up the other half of the blank we still want the common sides (black and white) against the vee block again with the center section towards the drill. You will notice that the grain alignment mark is now on the right side of the exposed surfaces. You will also notice that the black surface is now where the white surface was in the last picture and the white where the black was. If the drill bit is not centered, any error after drilling will be in the same direction for both pieces. You need to have the entire set-up solid and square in order to drill holes correctly. If it is set up correctly and your blanks are the same size, you can drill any number of blanks just by clamping them in and drilling.

I use a hand clamp to secure the blank to the vee block when I drill. This helps me drill a straighter hole because the wood is less likely to move than if I held it by hand. The wood on the bottom of the set-up also acts as a back up to help prevent blow out and protects the drill table if you drill too deep.

After drilling a hole or two, shavings will accumulate in the corner of the vee block. These shavings will not allow your common surfaces to seat properly. The shavings can be removed with a straw or piece of tubing stuck into the corner and given a good puff of air. Direct the air so the shavings don't blow back in your face.

Since you will not have a black side and a white side to help you place the blanks in the vee block with the correct orientation, line both sections of the blank up so the alignment mark is together. Then pull them down as if you were breaking a stick and place into the vee block using the common surfaces.

Notice the location of the alignment mark. This mark can also help you orient the blank correctly.

On the left is a standard twist drill bit. This is your normal metal working drill bit and will do quite a good job, but is susceptible to wandering.

The second from the left is a brad point with a long twist. This drill bit has a long point in the middle which is easy to set up, and cuts with the tips of the flutes leaving a very clean hole and clearing the wood chips from the hole quite well. This is one of my favorite drills.

The second from the right is a parabolic drill bit. It is very aggressive and cleans the chips from the hole extremely well. One of the downfalls of this drill is that it cuts so fast that, in hard material, when the drill breaks through the bottom, the work piece tends to climb the drill, sometimes breaking the blank.

The far right drill is a bullet drill bit. It also has a center point, but this one is heavier than the one on the brad point which is much more pointed. It drills with less deflection, ejects chips quite well, is not as aggressive as the parabolic, and does not have as severe a blow out. This is another of my favorites for Dymondwood or very hard woods.

When the flute tips are below the surface, apply pressure until you can feel the cutting action of the drill. You want to feel uniform pressure while cutting. If you push too hard, the cutting action is forced. If too little pressure is applied, the drill has a tendency to burnish the surface, create heat, and cut poorly. When you achieve the right feel of the cutting action, both the cut and the shavings will be clean. Since clean shavings remove the heat, the blank will be noticeably cooler after drilling. Drill in stages, raising the drill from the work piece occasionally to eject excess shavings from the hole. A build-up of chips on the flutes will create an undesirable binding and heat.

A blow out. Notice the ragged edges. Believe me, it can be worse. The blank can even crack down the side. The wooden block attached to the drill table provides something for you to drill into and will help prevent this. With some woods, even this does not provide a guarantee, and larger diameter holes are more susceptible to blow out.

If you have enough stock on the length of your blank, one way to avoid blow out is to mark the drill bit with tape, creating a depth stop. The depth of the hole should be slightly deeper than the depth required for the brass tube. Drill to your depth stop without going through the piece. Then trim off the end, which will leave a clean hole. You certainly do not need to follow this procedure all of the time, but it is a handy technique to know about for some materials and difficult grains.

As you gently bring down the drill, touch the work surface and allow the point to seek its center. No matter which type of drill you use, if you force it, or don't give it a chance to locate itself, the drill will have a tendency to skate in the direction of the least resistance. This tendency holds true until the tips of the flutes are below the surface.

TIP
I use small rubber bands to keep my pairs together when I am doing more than one pen at a time, a very simple technique that I like. You may, in time, develop a different way, such as the use of pegged racks, that will suit your needs.

Gluing

One of the most important aspects of pen making is the gluing of the brass tubes to the wood. Usually failures make the pen a piece of scrap. A number of steps can be taken to reduce the possibility of failure.

I use one of three kinds of glue depending on which materials I am working with.

1. Cyanoacrylate or super glue is the one most people use most often. Although this glue is not the cleanest to apply, as it sticks to your fingers and anything else it touches, it is my favorite. It cures immediately, and I can get penetration with it that I cannot get with any other glue. However, it does get brittle with age, and, if not applied correctly, will leave voids. The high heat of curing can also cause blisters if it puddles on your hands.

2. Two-part epoxy: I use both the 5 minute and the long term epoxies. Each has their place. The long term is the strongest with much longer working time, making it much more forgiving while it is being applied. However, because it takes longer to cure, you cannot continue to the next step as quickly. The 5-minute epoxy is still strong, but the working time before curing is much shorter, as is the wait

between the next step. Epoxy is not as brittle, and will fill a gap between the wood and the brass better than cyanoacrylate. On Dymondwood, Corian, and impregnated woods which tend to be smooth, I feel 2 part epoxy is superior to cyanoacrylate. Clean up is also much easier. With solvents, it wipes right off your hands before it cures.

3. Polyurethane: This is a new glue that I think has real merit in pen-making. It is waterproof, expands to fill gaps, doesn't creep, and again cleans up with mineral spirits. It is a one-part, straight from the tube glue that has all the qualities necessary for a good bond between the brass and the wood without any toxic fumes. Curing is not as fast as either cyanoacrylate or 5-minute epoxy, but still faster than long-term epoxy. I do not like to use this glue for metal to metal as other glues work better, but for gluing the tube to the wood, it is a very good choice.

Procedure

I use a double glue process when gluing the brass tube into the blank. I use the water thin glue to coat the inside of the wooden blank because many times there are cracks, loose knots, punky wood, or any of a multitude of defects that cannot be seen until we have reduced our diameter during turning. The water thin glue will run through the blank, enabling it to reach defects all the way through as the thicker glue cannot.

Immediately, before the glue cures, I partially insert the brass tube into the blank and coat with medium density glue and work it into both ends with a rotating motion before seating. This must be done quickly before either glue has a chance to set-up.

Using 220 or 320 sandpaper, clean the outside of the brass tubes. This eliminates most of the residue left from the lubrication used during their manufacture, and establishes a fresh, clean, and scored surface to help bond the glue.
If I am cleaning a number of tubes, I do it on the lathe. I insert a mandrel into the chuck, and with the lathe running, put a tube onto the end of the mandrel. The tube will spin on the mandrel so I only put it on about a quarter inch. With my finger I apply a little pressure on the unsupported end of the tube, which creates enough bind to lightly sand the tube. Do not apply too much pressure or it will distort the tube and prevent a good press fit of related parts at assembly.

TIP
To use cyanoacrylate to glue in the brass, place a sheet of wax paper on your work surface. The glue will not stick to wax paper. Be careful: while a puddle of glue will not cure on wax paper, it will cure on your hand should you lay your hand in it! Occasionally I hit the paper with the accelerator to cure the puddles.

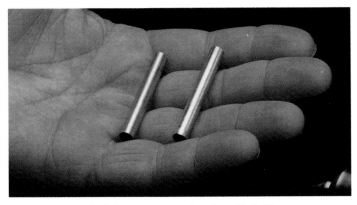

The tube on the left is not cleaned and scuffed. The one on the right is.

Note the smudge on the wood. This is how the super-thin glue penetrates through burl.

Coat the inside of the blank with the water thin glue. Moving quickly, insert the tip of the tube.

Apply medium density glue to the tube and roll and twist the tube in and out as far as you can while still retaining your hold on the tube. This coats the inside of the blank.

Pull out and reverse the blank, inserting the tube back into the hole at the end with the grain orientation,

and seat it for proper depth. This way, when we trim it all of the trimming will be at the far ends, providing for a better match where the two pieces are joined.

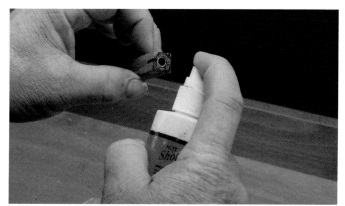

Spray on accelerator which cures the glue job instantly.

Turning

1. **Mandrels**: Before we can turn these pens we need a mandrel— a tool designed to be held in the head stock and supported by the tail stock to drive the work piece concentrically to the axis of the lathe. A drill chuck or a morse taper can hold it in the head stock. Mandrels can be designed to hold one or two barrels at a time, and can be either one- or two- piece. The single barrel mandrel is easier for a novice because the shorter length results in less deflection. The double mandrel allows you to turn both halves on the same set-up, but accurate alignment between the head stock and tail stock is absolutely essential because even a minor variation will be amplified at the tail stock end. Mandrels hold the stock in one of two ways: a one-piece mandrel normally uses a hand knob or nut to compress the barrels on the mandrel so that they can be driven. A two-piece uses the tail stock to apply the pressure. The two-piece is faster and easier to assemble or disassemble, but allows more deflection than the solid one piece mandrel. Choose your weapon.

2. **Bushings** are loose pieces that slide on the mandrels to provide a guide to establish the diameter of the pen or pencil barrels. Bushings can also be used to turn larger pens on smaller mandrels by

providing shoulders for the brass tubes. By using different bushings a mandrel can be used to make more than one style of pen or pencil.

3. **Tools:** the tool I use most for turning pens is the skew. It gives me a good clean-cut finish, is fast, and I feel comfortable with it. It also provides a uniform diameter cut rather than one with bumps and ridges. The second tool I use is a 3/8 or 1/4 inch spindle gouge. When the grain is especially prone to tearing, the gouge allows me to take a different type of cut, avoiding some of that tearing. Some woods and man-made materials are also easier to rough down with a gouge than a skew. Occasionally I use a very flat 3/4 inch roughing gouge which provides a compromise between the skew and the spindle gouges. I also use a 1/16 inch parting tool to cut shoulders and occasionally clean up the ends.

4. The ends of the blank are very prone to chipping or tearing, since the corners are 90 degree angles. Treat these with the same respect as if you were a nudist going through a barbed wire fence. With care. Sometimes you have to go against the normal rule to cut from the center toward the ends. Occasionally, you may have to gently come back against the ends toward the centers. This at times will prevent tearing or chipping.

5. Do not scrape. The thickness of the wood between the brass tube and the finished diameter is so thin that scraping tends to tear the section free from the tube which ruins the pen. Occasionally using a shear scrape with a spindle gouge will help on a troublesome area, but be careful!

TIP

I apply a light coat of tung oil finish to the mandrels and bushings occasionally. This helps to load the brass tubes easily. It also helps to keep the pen from bonding to the mandrel if you have used cyanoacrylate glue to patch a chip or crack and have gotten a little sloppy. It doesn't always work, but it helps. You could use a machine oil or wax, but these could contaminate the finish. The tung oil finish dries and eliminates this problem. If it builds up and creates binding, clean it off and start again.

---

6. When close to the finished diameter, some woods may be punky, porous, have a testy area, or cracks may develop, I sometimes coat the entire blank with water thin cyanoacrylate. This strengthens the grain, fills pores, seals cracks, and allows a pen that otherwise may have become scrap, to be finished. After the glue is cured, reduce the pen to the finished diameter.

7. Sharp tools are always very important, but even more so when working with wood of this thickness. If your tools are not sharp, you will tear the wood and will have to decrease the blank to a dimension which is too small to match the rest of your pen parts. Dull tools also increase the chance that you will tear the wood from the brass tube. The finishing will also be greatly improved with clean cuts.

8. Along with sharp tools, you need a light touch. Heavy handed or white-knuckled turning does not enter the picture for pens. This project requires finesse, especially with highly figured grain patterns, as you always seem to be cutting against the grain somewhere.

9. **Speed:** Since this project is working with a small diameter, the surface speed is relatively slower for the same lathe speed. The pen blank travels a much shorter distance to make one rotation than does a large bowl. Therefore, the lathe speed must be much faster to achieve the same surface speed for the pen as for a bowl. The exact speed you use will depend on your style, skills, and the materials you are using. If you set the lathe speed too slow, you will not get a clean cut. It will tend to tear the wood rather than slice it. If your speed is too great you will have burning, chattering, and loss of control. The majority of people believe that speed is the savior. However, too much is just as bad as too little.

Finishing

The main choices for finishing are oil, French Polish, wax, or compounds and buffing. My favorite is French Polish. It is a fast finish, is easy to apply, fills pores relatively easily, provides for a wide range of final surface conditions from matte to high gloss, and stands up quite well with use.

Oil finishes come with many different characteristics. Different brands use different additives and driers. Oil will penetrate and last well, but you cannot get a high gloss. It offers the advantage that it can be reapplied later in case of damage or wear to the pen.

Cloth wheels and compounds are needed for buffing. This process is used on Corian, Dymondwood, and other resin impregnated materials. The resins create their own finish, and the compounds and wheels polish the surface to remove scratches and surface blemishes and leave a high gloss.

Wax is easily applied, gives an initial luster, and is easily reapplied, but does not have the durability of other finishes. Wax can also be applied over one of the other finishes to create a higher polish. The best results from wax are achieved if it is applied with loose cloth wheels on a buffer. The wheel can also be mounted in the head stock of the lathe to hand buff the pen.

Assembly

Assembly is just as important as the turning and finishing. An arbor press is the best, but a vise or hand clamp can also be used. Whichever you use, be sure to use wooden jaws to protect the metal parts. If you don't have wooden jaws, you can tape wood to the metal jaws for the same protection.

Don't try to force the pen parts together. If it doesn't press in smoothly, stop to find out what is causing the problem. If you press the tube in at an angle, the wood will tend to crack. Press hard enough to solidly seat the parts, but not so hard that you will damage something.

Some metal to metal parts need to be glued. I glue anything that is threaded, because later twisting will place undue demands on the parts. I used to rely on pressing alone, but failures have occurred. Now I reinforce the pressing with glue and have had no failures since.

You can use super glue or two-part epoxy. Super glue is fast, but susceptible to mistakes. Parts may not be positioned correctly before the glue cures, and excess glue may be forced out onto the pen surface, damaging the finish. Normally one drop of medium-density glue inside the tube before the parts are pressed together is sufficient.

I prefer to use five-minute epoxy because I can correct misalignment and wipe off any glue which has been forced out. When gluing parts together, the epoxy acts as a lubricant, allowing the parts to go together easily. Sometimes hand pressure is sufficient when using epoxy, although you want to seat it to make sure that everything is tight.

Much more detail will be provided on assembly when we provide step-by-step instructions for construction of the twist pen, which will be our first project.

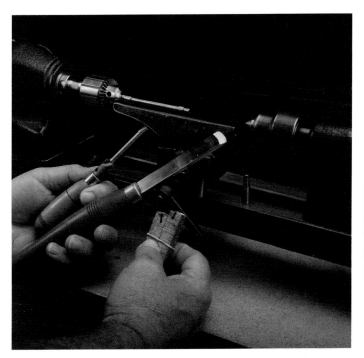

The set-up required to turn the twist pen: a two-piece 7 mm mandrel held in a drill chuck, a live center on the tail stock, a 3/4 " skew, a pen mill, and a pair of black ash burl pen blanks with the brass tubes glued in.

The pen mill is a very good tool to clean up the ends of the blank so that they are square to the axis of the tube. It also will clean any excess glue from inside the tube itself, not only by rotating, but also by using the end to push the glue from the tube. Insert the pen mill into the tube

and rotate it until the wood is even with the brass. Do both ends. Do not remove any more brass than is necessary to make a clean surface. The length of the blank can be important in some pens.

This clean, squared surface is required to provide a matching fit when the parts are assembled.

Here is the sequence used to load the blanks onto the mandrel: blank with the grain orientation mark in the center, center bushing, second blank with the marking in the center lined up with the mark on the first blank, and the end mandrel.

Bring up the tail stock and tighten. Apply only enough pressure to drive the assembly.

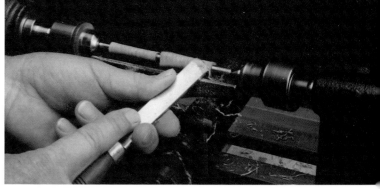

Repeat the same procedure on the other blank.

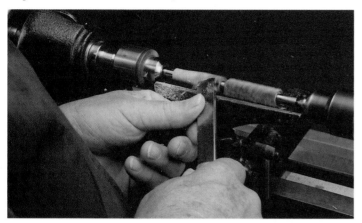

Clean up the blank using the skew, and reduce the diameter.

Reducing.

When you are reducing the square, start a short distance in from the ends and push off the corners. Continue cleaning up working toward the center. Repeat on the opposite side.

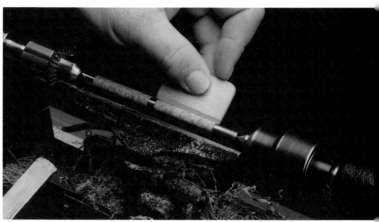

Match the diameter of the blanks to the bushing diameter (the diameter of the mandrel which you have matched to the diameter of the pen fittings).

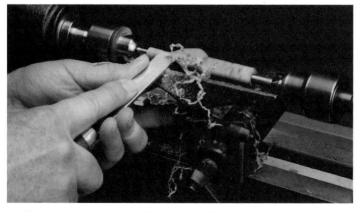

Continue to reduce the diameter until it is close to the bushing diameter.

To check for flatness between the bushings, I use a piece of hard maple with a straight edge. This piece of wood which I fashioned for this purpose works better than a 6" ruler which is too long to fit between the mandrels.

I also use a micrometer.

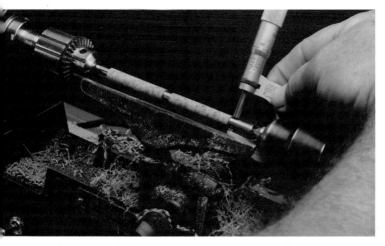

After mandrels have been used for a number of pens, the bushings and mandrel diameters will become somewhat reduced through wear from sanding. In order to have the pen parts fit exactly, the diameter of the blank needs to be slightly larger than that of the mandrel. Since the wood wears faster than the metal, you want the wood to be a couple thousandths proud of the metal parts. The micrometer makes it possible to achieve this precision by taking the guess work out of measuring a round object which is very difficult to measure any other way. Some people think that this step is overkill, but for a truly fine pen, this is necessary.

Continue to reduce the diameter.

Notice how I support the blank with my hand to cut down on chattering. I apply the same pressure with my fingers from the back as I apply with the skew from the front.

Do the same on the other blank.

Progress shot. If you use clean cuts, the surface will be clean, uniform, and ready for sanding. The cleaner the cuts the less you will need to sand.

Will you look at those shavings! I love it!

To give myself sanding pieces which are easy to use, I cut a full piece of sandpaper into sixths. Then I fold these pieces into thirds. This provides a size which is easy to hold, stiff enough to sand with, and has lots of edges to sand up against detail without rolling the edges. I use the same arrangement for all my sanding. My sandpaper sequence is 180, 220, 320, and 400. I prefer silicone carbide paper as the grit is white and does not leave dark residue in the pores like wet and dry paper will on light woods.

TIP
The type of sanding paper you use can have a dramatic effect on your finished pen or project. I prefer to use white silicone carbide paper when sanding my pens. Even though wet and dry paper is available in finer grits, since it is black, it will leave its dark residue in the pores of the wood. With light colored wood, it will discolor the wood and leave a muddy appearance.

With the lathe stopped, use the 400 grit sandpaper lengthwise with the grain to eliminate concentric sanding rings.

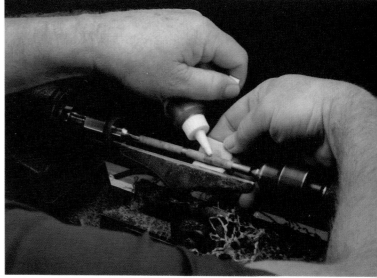

For this pen we are using French Polish, a fast drying padding lacquer. I transfer some polish from the large container to a smaller one which is easy to use, and since exposure to air causes the polish to thicken, it keeps the remainder usable for a longer period of time. A rag can be used to apply the polish, but I prefer to use shot gun patches. These can be folded into quarters, making a perfect size for my purposes. They are lint free, cheap, and disposable. After I have used the patch several times, the dried polish build-up provides an excellent base for the polish, allowing me to apply the finish much faster.

Sanding. Work through your grits, 180 through 400, with the lathe running.

For the initial application of polish, saturate the blank while the lathe is running, rather than putting the polish on the patch. The pores of the blanks hold a lot of dust particles. If you put the polish on the patch instead of the blank itself, these dust particles will get a coat of finish over them. By saturating the blank, the dust particles absorb the polish as well and do not leave blemishes on the wood. This gives a uniform finish.

On light woods I use a relatively clean patch when I am saturating the wood with the initial coat. If I were to use a patch that had been used with dark wood such as cocobolo which bleeds its color into the patch, this residue can wash into the pores of the lighter wood. This can cause a stained or mottled finish instead of the clear wood color we are striving for.

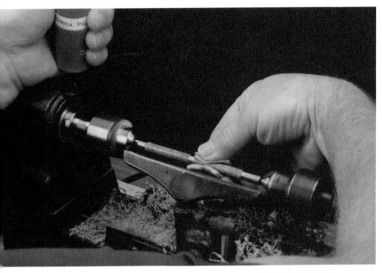

After the initial saturation, continue to build the finish by putting the French Polish on the pad and then applying it to the work.

Continue until you have the desired finish.

If you look carefully, you may see some dark rings on the blank on the right. These rings are a common problem, created by a build-up of polish. The build-up is usually caused by failure to keep the patch moving evenly back and forth while polishing or by applying to much pressure. The eraser: 0000 steel wool. With the lathe running remove the rings. You only need to remove the rings; you do not need to remove all of the polish. It does not hurt to work in the direction of the grain, again with the lathe stopped. Apply polish again until you are satisfied with the finish. If you need to rework the finish on one half, do the same on the other half to keep the finish uniform. Even if one half does not have rings, refinish it.

When removing the blanks from the mandrel, we have to keep track of our grain orientation. When we turned the pen, we lost the original orientation marks that we were using earlier. When I remove the blanks from the mandrel, I hold them so that the outer ends, those positioned to the outside of the mandrel, are pointing up.

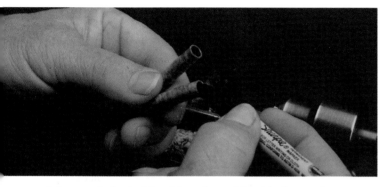

I then mark the inside of the tubes with a felt tip pen. I move the markings from the center of the pen to the ends of the pen because the fittings on the ends will cover the marks.

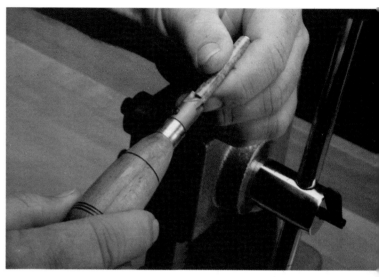

Using the pen mill, lightly remove any finish build-up, so that a nice clean surface to mate to our metal parts remains. Be careful not to crack the wood. You should not be removing wood, only excessive finish.

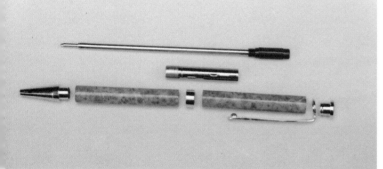

The parts of the pen ready for assembly.

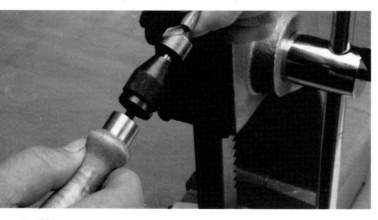

I like to countersink the brass tube slightly. I break the inside corners of the brass so that the mating metal parts have no interference.

Inspect the two blanks to decide which end should be at the top and which the bottom. If you have a chip or a minor imperfection at one end, choose this for the top because the clip may cover it. Normally I place the best grain on the bottom where the view of the wood is unimpeded by the clip. We insert the writing tip into the end of the bottom blank and press together with the arbor press or vise. Make sure you have wooden jaws or covers.

The tip is now seated.

Press.

I made a wooden vee block from hardwood maple to establish the depth of the twist mechanism so the ink refill will fit properly. The ends must be square and thick enough so that it sits solidly on a press or in a vise. If it does not sit flatly on the base of the press, you will not be able to insert the twist mechanism without binding. Mine is 3 and 15/16ths inches long. You may want to start at 4" and adjust the length to your liking. If you make it too short, the mechanism will not retract the refill inside the pen.

Insert the refill and tighten down, making sure the twist mechanism is in its open position. Check to make sure that the refill protrudes to your satisfaction. If it does not protrude far enough, shave a little off the length of the vee block. This will make a shorter mechanism assembly, which will make the refill tip protrude farther. If it protrudes too far already, you need to make a new vee block.

Put the center ring over the twist mechanism and then put the twist mechanism into the other half of the blank. Since the center ring is the same diameter as the blank, by putting the ring on the twist mechanism first, it will help keep everything aligned while pressing together.

Assemble the cap and the clip with the top of the blank, remembering to check for the marking in the end of the barrel. Rotate the clip to cover imperfections or poor grain.

Press.

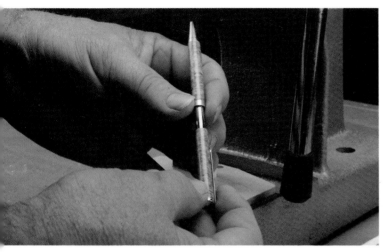

Retract the refill, align the grain for the two parts, and push the parts together. Now when the pen is closed the grain will be in proper alignment.

The finished pen.

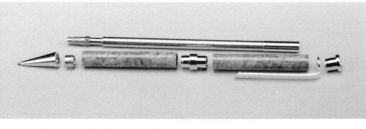

The parts for the pencil.

The initial steps for the pencil are the same as those for the pen, from the seating of the brass tubes in the blanks, to the turning and finishing of the blanks.

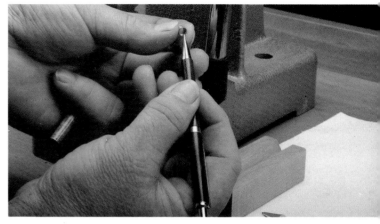

The tip end bushing has a recessed diameter on one side. Place this side into the pencil tip end of the blank and press.

Countersink the brass tube and remove any excess finish as you did on the pen.

Note that the tip bushing is pressed flush to the end of the blank.

Check for grain alignment marks to identify the top of the pen. Take the center connector and insert it into the top of the bottom blank and the bottom of the top blank and align the grain. Do this now; after they are pressed together, it is one unit.

Slide the pencil mechanism into the top of the pen.

I use the vee block to align the two while pressing to keep the pencil straight. This is very important because, if the assembly of these two halves are not in perfect alignment, the pencil mechanism will not function properly. The vee block is used only for alignment and not to measure depth as it is with the pen.

If this does not assemble freely, the mechanism will stick and not function properly. This is the biggest problem with the pencil, but can be avoided if you make sure it is aligned properly at all stages.

Attach the cap and the clip to the barrel assembly. Position the clip to your liking as you did with the pen, and press.

Screw on the tip.

The finished pencil.

The set.

Heavier Twist Pen

Variation on the Standard Twist Pen

For those who like a heavier pen, the standard twist mandrel and pen kit can be used, but the center bushing or gold center ring provided by the kit can be replaced to allow for a pen body with a larger diameter. For this demonstration, we will create our own center ring out of pic-guard or plastic spacer material and the pen will rotate on this surface to open or close. A contrasting wood could also be used although wood is susceptible to splitting.

The pen blanks (these are cocobolo) have been drilled, glued and cleaned with the pen mill, as described for the standard twist pen. they are now ready to turn.

Notice that the pic-guard material is placed between the blanks in place of the center bushing for the last pen. We will establish our own center diameter. The end diameters must still match the end bushing size so that the related pen parts still match.

I am using .090 pic-guard material, used in guitar making, for the center ring. I found the center and drilled a whole just big enough to fit over the twist mechanism. A 1/4" drill will do this, but a number F drill provides a little clearance.

Start to reduce the square to a round diameter. Reduce the end diameters from a center direction,

Use a counter sink to de-burr both sides of the plastic.

gradually working back toward the center.

Notice that I am reducing the pic-guard as well. As we reduce the center diameter, the diameter of the pic-guard will decrease to the same diameter as that created by the pen mill in the blanks--the largest diameter you can use for the center of the pen. Since the end of the blanks have been holding the pic-guard in place, when you reduce the center diameter to the diameter of the cleaned, pen milled surface, the pic-guard will become loose. You must now tighten the tail stock to hold the pic-guard in place.

Continue to shape the pen.

The Pen mill hole.

Stop the lathe periodically and check the shape, form, and surface for defects.

The diameter of the plastic matches the center diameter of the blank. This is as large a pen as we can make using the pen mill.

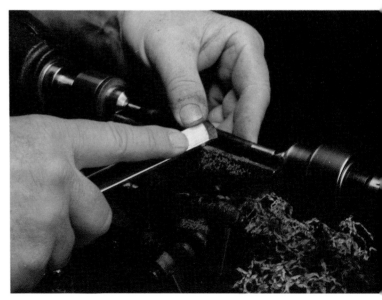

Refine your shape with a light touch until you are satisfied.

Sand with the lathe running, working in progression through your grits, starting with the 180 right through to the 400.

Complete the final sanding with the lathe stopped, using the 400 in the direction of the grain to remove sanding rings.

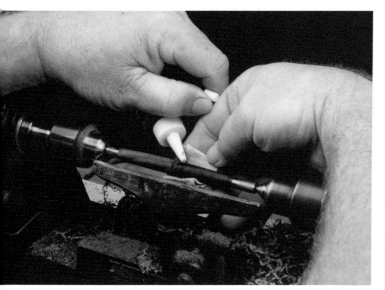

Finish using the French Polish. Again, saturate the wood first, and then apply further polish with the patch. To get a really nice finish on cocobolo, it takes numerous applications of polish. With 0000 steel wool, remove excess polish from the surface between applications. This will help to fill the pores for a smoother surface.

Assemble the same way we did the original twist pen, using the vee block to establish the depth of the twist mechanism. The only change is the use of the plastic in place of the gold center ring. I used a chrome kit to accent the burgundy red of the cocobolo.

The pen put together.

Note the increased diameter of the pen on the right. These two pens are made from the same kits except for the substitution of the plastic center ring and the chrome finish.

Golf Pen

Variation on the Standard Twist Pen

Another variation on the regular twist pen kit is the Golf Pen.

The only difference in the kit is the clip which is a miniature golf club. I am also going to add diagonal black and white stripes which I will make from pic-guard material for an extra feature. Wood or another material which will provide a contrasting color can be used for this insert. I have chosen fiddleback myrtle for the blank as this will contrast nicely with the stripes.

Mark a line for grain orientation.

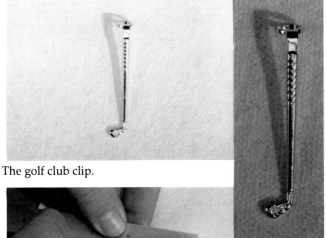

Use a blank slightly longer than the pen parts. Draw a centerline to determine the middle of your pen.

Make sure that both surfaces of the cut are clean and uniform to each other. I use a disc sander.

The golf club clip.

When sanding the blank, sand one edge of the insert to match the angle.

About 3/4 of an inch from the center line mark the location of the beginning of the stripe. I cut mine using an angle of 45 to 50 degrees, starting at this point. The angle and exact location are a matter of choice. Saw along this line.

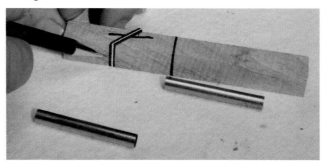

This will form an even surface when we glue in the insert. If this is not done, we may develop a void when our pen is turned.

Use the vee block to align the pieces on two common surfaces while you glue. You will want to line the vee block with wax paper. Since super glue does not adhere to wax paper you will be able to remove the blank from the vee after gluing.

If the insert is man-made material, rough up both sides to increase adhesion. Then glue the pieces together, making sure that all surfaces are coated.

Hold the sides flat in the vee and tight together, hit with accelerator.

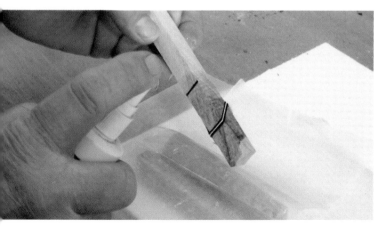

Wait a minute. Remove from wax paper and hit the other sides with accelerator. We now have a blank with a stripe.

The two sides which were in the vee block are now your common sides. Using these common sides and the center line mark, cut your blank sizes. Proceed with drilling, inserting the tubes and cleaning up the ends as described for the standard twist pen.

Turn the blanks exactly as you turned the blank for the standard twist pen.

You can turn the blank with the stripe just as you would turn a regular blank.

The pen is now ready for finishing,

and assembly. The miniature golf club clip and those ubiquitous golf stripes climbing the side sure draw the golfers.

Corian® Pen

No need to worry about matching the grain on Corian. There is none. Cut your blanks, drill them, and clean them as described previously.

As the diameter decreases, support the blank from behind, just as you do the wooden blanks.

Corian turns very much like wood, although it does require more pressure.

All this was done with the skew.

Because there is no grain, it makes long ribbons.

Sand the same way you sand wood.

Corian sure does create a beautiful mess!

The other wheel is a loose cloth wheel. Use white rouge on the wheel

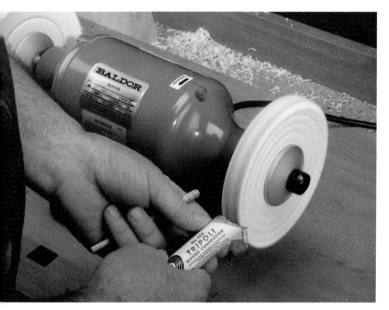

To finish, I am using a 3600 rmp buffer with 6 inch wheels. One wheel is a concentric sewn cloth wheel which is a little harder and has a more aggressive cutting action. On this wheel, I use Tripoli compound.

and with the work piece again held at an angle, polish to a fine luster.

This combination removes scratches from sanding and does the major portion of the polishing. I put the blank on a dowel to make it easier to hold and buff the blank at an angle.

Finished corian pen. We used a double bead center ring. My favorite answer to people who ask about these pens is, "They are for Chevrolet truck drivers--like a rock."

Dome-Top Pen

I am Using cocobolo wood because it is one of the most attractive and best selling woods I have.

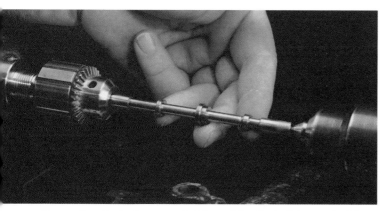

I am using the 2 piece mandrel I used for the twist pens, but I have added a set of bushings for the Dome-Top pen. Here I have a bushing in the middle and one at each end. Each of these bushings has a different diameter, which establishes the shape of the pen.

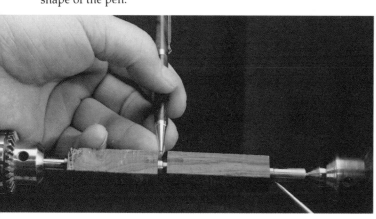

The blank must have a minimum width of 5/8" square, which is larger than those we used for the twist pens, to accommodate the larger Dome-Top hardware. Cut the blanks, drill them, and clean up the ends with the mill.

Reduce the bottom half of the pen to the diameter of the bushings.

Reduce the top half to match those bushings. The curvatures between the bushings are free formed.

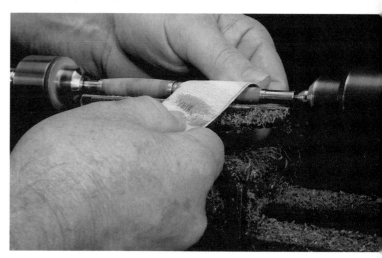

Sand.

Sanded ready for finish.

French polish has just been applied as a finish.

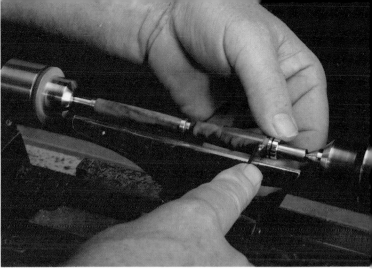

Holding the center ring between the fingers of my left hand, go in with a parting tool to cut a tenon which matches the inside diameter of the ring. The diameter is achieved through trial and error.

Switch the blanks so that the top of the pen is on the right, so that you can fit the center ring. At this point, the bushings are used only as spacers, so that you can drive the pen. I have left the tip bushing on the tail stock end here because it is small enough for the center ring to pass over it while fitting the ring.

Once the correct diameter for the tenon is established near the end, move the shoulder back, maintaining the tenon diameter. This keeps it concentric to the outside diameter of the pen. We continue making successive light cuts until the end of the ring is flush with the end of the tenon.

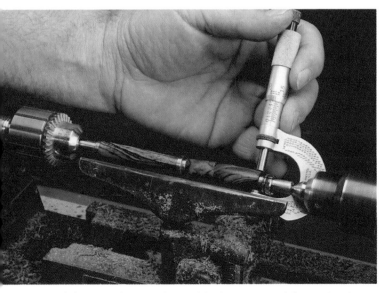

While I was shaping the top blank, I was careful to maintain the diameter of the barrel to at least the width of the center ring.

If these steps are done correctly the fit will be like this. I proceed through the steps in this order is because it is easier to size the tenon to the center ring when the blanks are reversed. By sanding and finishing the blanks before cutting the tenon, the shoulder is sharp and matches the center ring. Sanding later may accidentally create a rounded edge.

Remove the center ring from the mandrel so it does not become damaged. Now apply a light coat of finish to the very edge of the shoulder to ensure that no raw wood shows if the surface is proud of the center ring. Do not finish the tenon as the polish would impair the bond when gluing the ring to the wood.

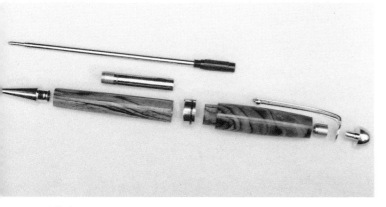

All the parts ready to assemble.

Press the tip into the end of the blank first to make sure it is solidly seated before you press the twist mechanism. If you press the two at the same time, the twist mechanism may press easier than the tip and the tip would be unable to seat properly.

Since the twist mechanism and refill are the same dimensions as those used for the standard twist pen, we can use the vee block for proper depth in this assembly. Press the twist mechanism in now. Install refill.

Place the cap nut into the top of the barrel, making sure the chamfered edge goes in first. Notice the line which defines the chamfer.

Seat the cap nut until it is flush with the top of the pen.

The instructions for the pen assembly direct you to assemble the cap, the clip and the cap nut together as a unit. I follow the sequence shown here so that I can position the clip to my best advantage. Using five minute, two-part epoxy, put a light coat on the wood on the end of the barrel,

33

and a light coat on the top of the clip.

and seat the center ring.

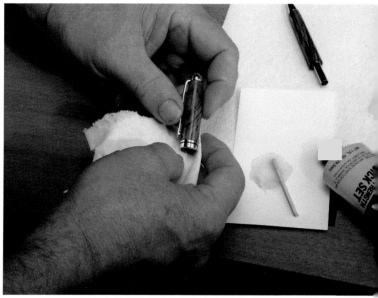

Install the cap through the clip and thread into the cap nut. Position the clip to accent your most attractive grain or to hide defects and tighten down. I glue mine because the glue will hold the clip in a permanent position. Without glue the clip can rotate or the cap can come off.

Wipe off the excess glue.

Apply a light coat of glue to the tenon you created for the center ring,

Close the twist mechanism and align the grain so the top and bottom match. Push the parts together. The Dome-Top pen.

Rollerball and Fountain Pen

I am using walnut burl. An elegant pen should have an elegant wood. This pen can be assembled as a rollerball or fountain pen. Only the tips and cartridges are different.

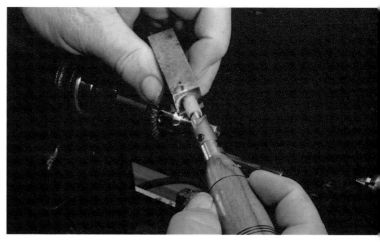

I am using a 10 mm single barrel two-piece mandrel, so I will be turning only one barrel at a time. These mandrels were designed specifically for this style of pen. Prepare the blanks as described for the twist pen.

When this bushing which we have created is used with the 7 mm pen mill, it allows us to trim our ends 90 degrees to the axis. The same technique can be used whenever the diameter of the tube is different from the pen mill.

Insert the tubes and clean up the ends, as with the twist pens.

The shaft of the pen mill is the diameter of the inside of a 7 mm tube. The brass tube for the rollerball is 10 mm, so we have to make a bushing. Take a 5/8" square hardwood blank such as maple and drill for a 7 mm brass tube. Glue in the tube. Use a set of 7 mm mandrels (regular pen mandrels) and turn the diameter down until it is a slip fit on the inside of the 10 mm brass tube.

As always, use a felt tip pen to mark the grain alignment.

Reduce the blank, as you did with the twist pens,

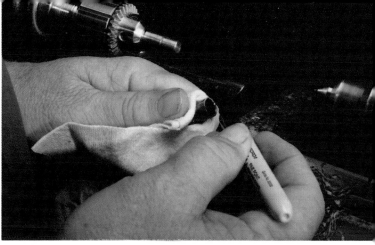

Mark the outside end of the pen. Again this is the opposite end from the center alignment mark shown earlier. The marks will be covered by the pen parts.

Until the diameter matches that of the mandrels.

Repeat the same procedure on the other blank.

Sand.

Rather than relying on a straight edge to make sure that the tubes match the bushings, I use a micrometer.

Finish with French Polish.

The parts for the rollerball pen.

The parts for the fountain pen.

The only parts that have changed are the tip, cartridge, and spring. The fountain pen parts are above those for the rollerball pen.

I prefer to use a file to cut this notch, although a dremel tool or small grinder will do the same. My choice for the file is a 6" bastard, because the width is close to that of the clip and it cuts swiftly. When filing this notch, always file towards the tube in a smooth cut. If you pull back, you have a tendency to chip the wood from the brass. Let the file do the cutting. When you have filed through the wood and the brass enough to fit the clip, you are ready to glue and assemble.

Choose which of the two blanks you would like to be on the top of the pen and which on the bottom. Then set the hardware for the pens in the position they will be assembled to help keep them in order.

Apply two-part epoxy to the inside of the tube and

You will need to cut a notch in the top to make room for the clip which is set below the cap mating surface.

a light coating on the wood at the end of the tube.

Align the clip assembly to the notch

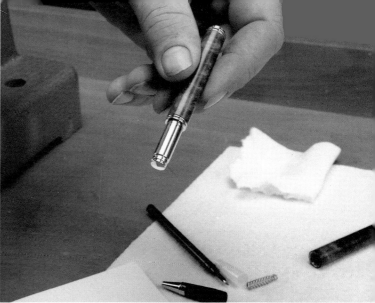

Screw on the end cap.

and press to seat. Wipe off any excess glue.

Drop in the spring, small end first.

Put a little glue on the inside of the tube and the end of the tube for both ends of the blanks, press in the threaded couplers, and press to seat, remembering grain orientation. Wipe off the excess glue and allow to cure.

Put in the refill.

Screw on the writing nib. The bottom half is complete.

With a phillips head screw driver, insert the plastic closing cap to the screw in the clip assembly, and adjust until the cap and the barrel fit tightly.

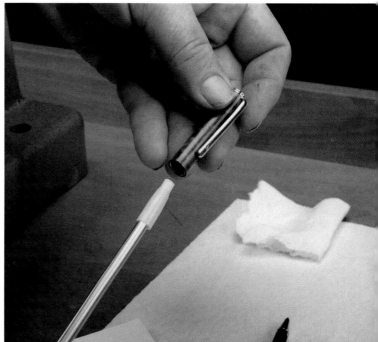

Finished.

Cigar Pen

I selected koa wood, native to Hawaii, for this project because it has iridescent qualities which really stand out with a larger pen. We have to start with a blank at least 3/4" square with length determined by the kit.

Occasionally you may want to try a new type of pen. Rather than investing in bushings, you may want to test the design by making it without bushings. I am going to make this pen without bushings to show how it can be done, although bushings are available for this pen style.

Cut drill and glue the blanks as previously described. Since this pen uses 10 mm tubes, you must also use your homemade bushings with the pen mill to square your ends. Square the ends carefully. If too much is taken off, the refill will not retract into the pen. The brass tube establishes the length of the blank because it defines the distance between the tip and the coupling which holds the twist mechanism.
All the parts are laid out in their proper relationship here.

We are using a 10mm, single blank, two-piece mandrel. Put your sketch where you can refer to it as you work. Put your blank in the mandrels, remembering the grain orientation mark.

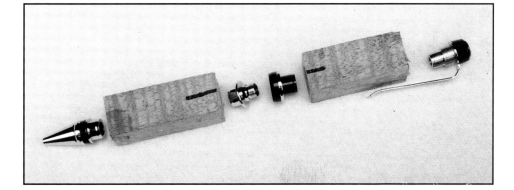

Sketch the pen with the diameters on the ends of the mating metal parts. Lay the pieces out in the order they will be assembled. A micrometer will provide the most accurate measurements. Check the mating diameter for each part and mark it on your sketch. Our blanks will have to be turned to these diameters at the established points, and contoured between as if we were using bushings.

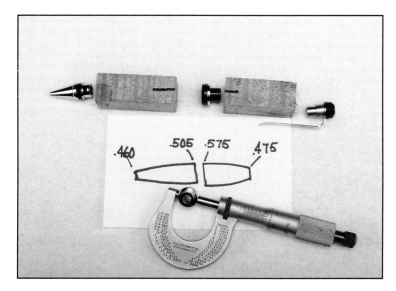

Reduce the blank, stopping frequently to check dimensions so that you do not remove too much stock. Blend the points between the two ends to create a pleasing contour.

If anything, leave the outer surface a touch proud of the pen mill surface, which will provide for a tight fit to the mating parts.

Both ends are now within .008 of the sketch dimensions. You need this extra for sanding.

Since we do not have bushings, while sanding, be very careful of the edges. The bushings help maintain the sharpness of the corners. Continue sanding, progressing through the grits as shown before.

Since the pen blank is a larger diameter than the pen mill, we need to true-up this surface manually.

Finish with French Polish. Then lightly clean up the excess finish on the end with a parting tool. The pen mill cannot do it on this larger diameter surface.

Using a small parting tool, clean that surface up 90 degrees to the center line.

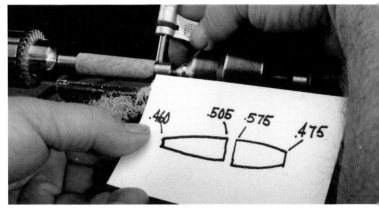

Repeat the process for the other blank. Again check the dimensions against the sketch.

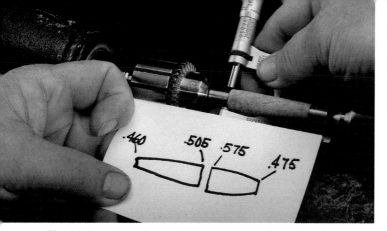

Check often. Once the stock is gone, it can't be replaced.

Put a little glue on the inside of the coupling end and a little on the end of the wood and insert the coupling.

Sand and use French Polish. The blank for the bottom of the pen is finished.

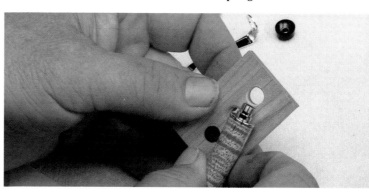

We must use a block of wood with a clearance hole

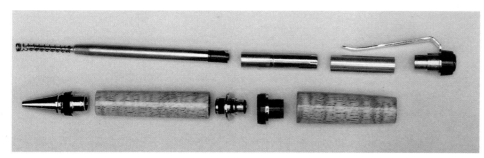

The parts for the cigar pen.

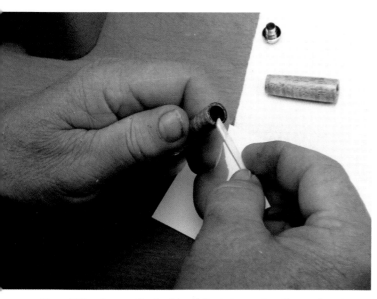

Put a little glue on the inside of the tube and on the end and press in the writing nib.

so that we can press against the coupling shoulder rather than the threaded end to avoid damaging the threads.

Using the block of wood again, put a little glue on the inside of the small brass tube and press in the cap nut, pressing against the shoulder of the nut rather than the threads.

Loosely assemble the clip parts. Put a little glue on the inside of the brass tube and the end grain and partially press together.

Align the clip where you want it, tighten the cap nut and press together. Allow to cure.

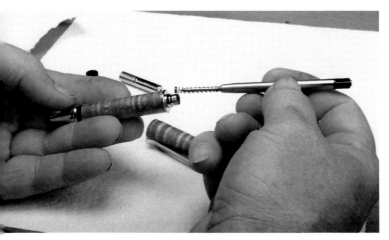

Put the spring on the end of the refill.

Put the twist mechanism over the refill and tighten it to the coupling.

The center ring slides in by hand

and with the grain aligned, the top gets pushed onto the twist mechanism to create a finished pen.

Flat-Top Click Pen

While all of the previous pens used a twist mechanism to propel the refill, this pen uses a click mechanism. Precise dimensions are more important on this pen. A number of the procedures I use will help make this pen work smoothly.

I am using desert ironwood. This is a hard, pretty wood with iridescent qualities. A one-piece mandrel and related bushings are used.

Reduce the diameter of both blanks. Care must be taken with ironwood, as it is brittle and chips easily. Note the flying chips.

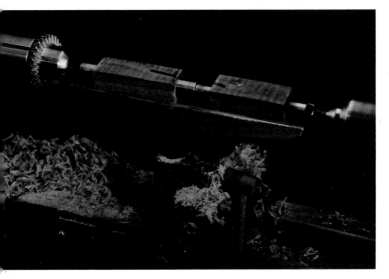

The blanks have been prepared as they were in previous instructions. The bottom brass again establishes the relationship of the refill to the clicker. If the length of the brass tube is shortened too much, the refill will not retract.

Before you establish the diameter of the top of your bottom barrel, verify the diameter of the holder for the click mechanism. You do not want the wood to be higher than this surface because both the wood and the click holder slide inside the brass of the upper barrel.

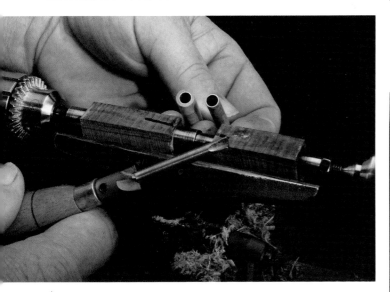

I had to make two new bushings for the pen mill, one for the top barrel and one for the bottom. I sized them to provide a slip fit to the inside of the brass tube. Again, this is important to square off the end of the blanks with the pen mill for a proper fit.

You need to match the bushing size on the bottom of the lower blank to fit the tip.

Sand the blanks and finish with French Polish.

Next, we must cut enough wood off the bottom end of the top barrel to accommodate the center ring.

The remaining wood will measure 1 and 3/4". The design specifies that the center ring is to be pressed onto the brass without the need for glue. When you press this ring on the brass, it compresses the inside diameter of the brass tube. This interferes with the ability of the bottom tube to slide inside during the click action. I remove a little of the outside diameter of the brass, which means that I must glue on the ring, but I do not compress the tube.

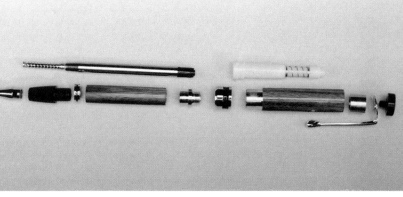

Parts for the click pen.

If the center ring cannot be slid on by hand without a lot of pressure, sand the exposed tube, being careful not to mar the wood,

Until the ring slides on well with hand pressure.

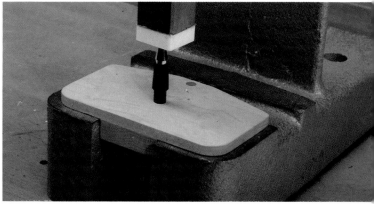

Press the tip into the nib assembly.

Add the trim ring.

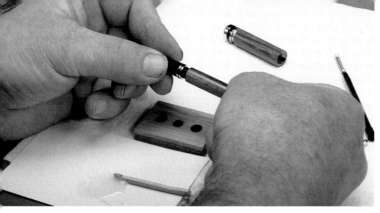

Apply a little glue to the inside and end of bottom tube. Insert nib assembly and seat.

Put a little glue inside the tube (not on the end), insert the clip bushing with the large diameter hole and seat flush with the top of the tube.

Apply a little glue to the inside of the top of the bottom tube, insert the click holder,

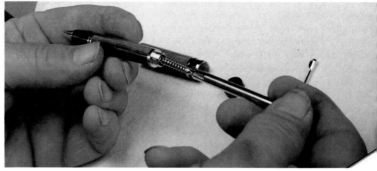

Put the spring and the refill in the bottom barrel.

and seat using a block of wood with a hole, so you press against the shoulder and do not damage the threads.

Put the click mechanism over the end of the refill and screw it down to the mechanism holder.

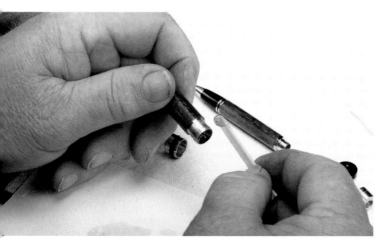

Put glue on the exposed brass tube, twist the center ring on, and wipe off excess glue.

Insert the cap over the click mechanism and press the top to make sure the top barrel moves freely over the bottom when the click mechanism is activated.

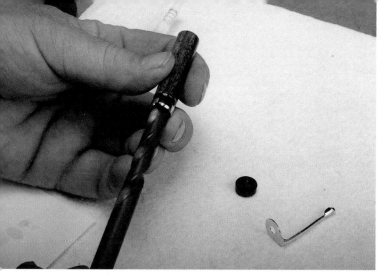

If binding occurs, stop. A letter X drill has a diameter which is very close to that of the inside of the brass tube. If you have compressed the inside diameter, insert the X drill by hand and rotate. Since the brass is soft, the drill will remove a small amount of brass, or if there is glue or another foreign residue blocking the tube, the drill should remove it. If it does not, a piece of dowel with sand paper wrapped around it can be inserted and used to polish the inside of the tube.

a drop on the threads, and assemble loosely. When we replace the refill, the click mechanism will unscrew, so make sure that the grain alignment depends on that position. Align the cap to the barrel grain, position your clip where you want it, while holding everything secure, tighten the finial. Wipe away excess glue.

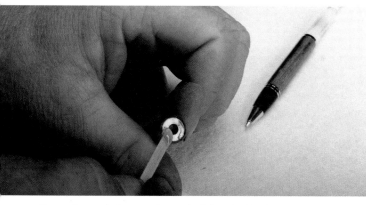

Put a drop of glue on the end of the clip bushing,

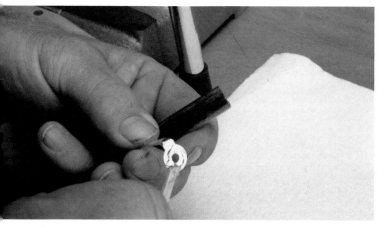

between the finial and the clip,

We have a click pen.

Flat-Top Twist Pen

I am using Dymondwood cut on a diagonal to show off its varied colors. For a totally different effect, the Dymondwood can be used with the laminations running parallel. Diagonal cut blanks are more difficult to turn because of the ever present end grain. You will always cut with the grain on one side of the blank and against the grain on the other. When you cut against the grain, your tool will tend to lift the laminations which are very thin, causing chipping. Sharp tools and a light touch are mandatory. The beauty of the finished pen can be well worth the extra effort.

You can either buy the blanks pre-cut or cut them yourself. Instructions for cutting and gluing the Dymondwood are available from suppliers of the wood. If you cut and glue your own diagonal pattern, you can alter the angle of the cut, you can double cut it, or you can use multiple cuts to create your own patterns. The patterns are only limited by your imagination.

Parallel lamination is on the top; the diagonal cut which we will be turning is cut, drilled, glued, trimmed, mounted on a one-piece mandrel with the Flat-Top twist-style related bushings. Ready to go.

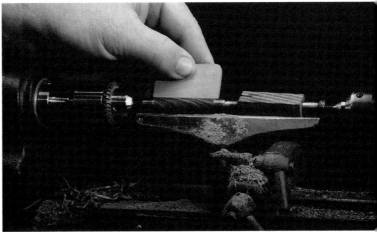

Check between the bushings to make sure the blank is reduced to the bushing diameter evenly, creating a parallel line. Notice the difference between the unturned blank and the turned one. Dymond and a Dymond in the rough.

Reduce the blanks with a light touch.

Turning is completed and we're ready to sand.

Sand as described previously. Mark the outer ends of the blanks to keep track of the grain orientation as we remove the blanks from the mandrels.

Finish buffing on the loose cloth wheel, with white rouge, again holding the piece at an angle. Notice that I am using a dowel to help control the handling of the blank. We do not need to use a finish on Dymondwood because the wood itself is so impregnated that buffing alone will provide a beautiful luster.

Murphy's law. I forgot to provide for the center ring. This step is normally done after sanding. Doing this step after buffing has a certain advantage as the sharpness of the corner might have been lost during buffing. The disadvantage is that the parts have to be reassembled on the mandrel. With a small parting tool remove the wood to the brass tube at the center of the pen on the top blank for the center ring. Take light successive cuts until the wood remaining measures 1 and 13/16" or use the template supplied with the mandrel. Use care not to chip the wood. Only go to the brass; do not decrease the brass diameter as this ring is designed to be pressed on.

Use the concentric sewn wheel with Tripoli. Holding the blanks at an angle, buff the blanks to remove the sanding marks. At an angle, the sanding marks will be removed more quickly and uniformly.

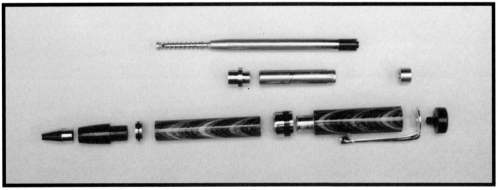

The set up for the Flat-Top twist pen.

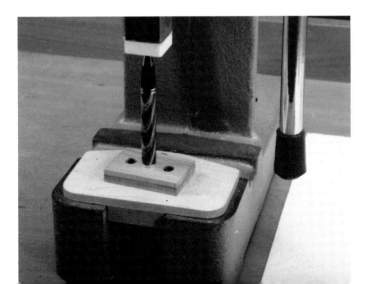

The bottom half is assembled in the same way as the Flat-Top click pen: press in the nib assembly and glue and press the twist mechanism, making sure to use the wooden block with the clearance hole to press the shoulder, thereby protecting the threads.

Press on the center ring. You do not need to glue this piece.

Apply glue to the end of the blank, between the cap nut and the clip, loosely assemble, select the position of your clip, tighten down the cap nut, and clean up any glue which has squeezed out.

Press in the clip bushing. (Gluing is an option which I prefer.) Seat flush with the end of the pen.

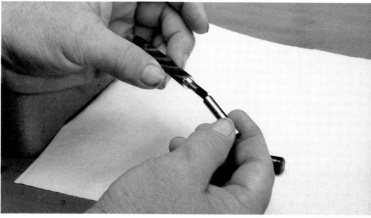

Insert the spring and the cartridge and screw the twist mechanism onto the threaded holder.

The pen.

Desk Pen

I am using bocote wood also know as Mexican rosewood. This pen is a variation of the twist pen which requires that we drill a blind hole in a long piece while still maintaining grain alignment. I am using a standard twist pen kit.

Insert the other half of the blank in the vee block, using the same common surfaces and orientation marks and drill through.

Create a set-up with the drill press table, vee block, and hand clamps to hold the blanks for drilling. Mark the center point and clamp the long blank into the vee block. Position the center of the blank in the vee block, using a drill or center point for positive location. I made my set-up on the side of the table so that the long blank could hang over, allowing me to use one set-up for both halves.

Put water thin super glue on the inside of the blank to seal possible cracks; invert and tap out the excess before it cures.

Since we are drilling a blind hole, we need to mark the drill with a piece of tape identifying a depth slightly longer than the length of the brass tube. With two common surfaces on the inside of the vee block, drill the long blank to the depth of the tape marking the drill.

Immediately insert the tip of the brass tube and apply medium super glue to the brass tube. Rotate to coat the tube evenly and seat.

Spray with accelerator. Repeat these steps on the other blank.

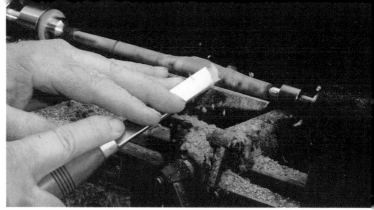

Move the tool rest to the long end of the pen and repeat the rounding.

I am again going to create my own center ring on this pen so I can increase the contour on the pen. I am using the long half of a double, two-piece mandrel, as this will support both blanks, and a drilled piece of pic-guard material for the center ring. In developing a shape, the only critical dimension is at the tip end. You also need to remember the length of the tube in the long section because you cannot reduce the dimensions in this section beyond that which is necessary to maintain structural strength.

When you have reduced the full length to a good base diameter, note the length of the brass tube insert by measuring the length on the blank and marking.

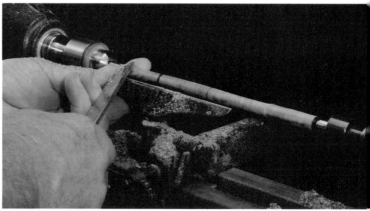

Refine the shape of the lower end of the pen.

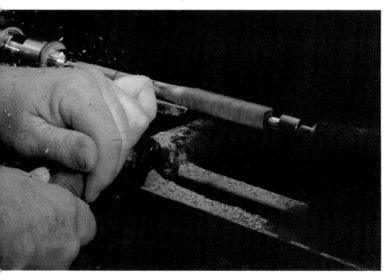

Start to turn the blanks, reducing the edges to create rounded surfaces.

Refine the shape at the upper end.

Adding an interesting end.

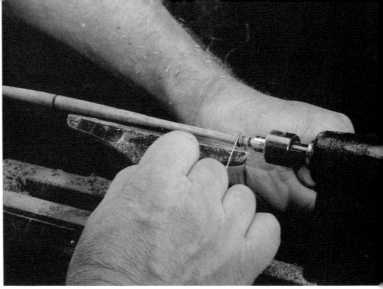

Sand.

I hold this in the groove with enough pressure to create friction. The friction causes heat; the heat burns the wood leaving black lines in the groove. Because the tip is thinner, than normal burn areas, I apply less pressure for a longer duration. An oily wood such as bocote will not burn as easily as do less oily woods like maple or walnut.

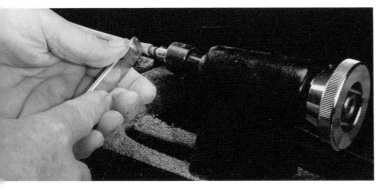

Stand the skew on end and use the long point to inscribe 2 lines. These lines are to install decorative burn marks with a wire. They will help hold the wire until it burns a groove. Without these marks, the wire has a tendency to skate from the desired location.

Progress.

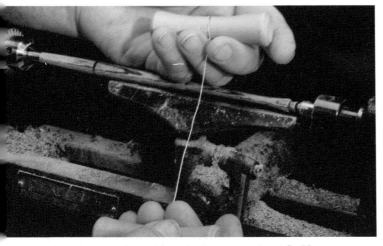

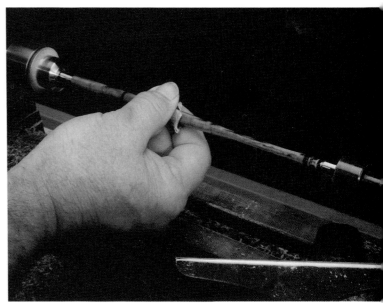

I have fashioned a mild steel wire, approximately 20 gage, with two wooden handles.

Finish with French Polish.

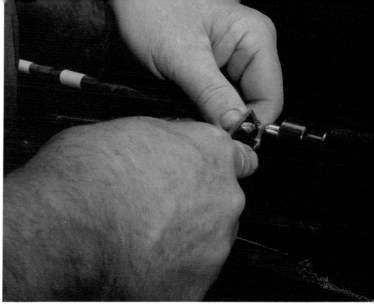

Tape the center ring and the tip section to the mandrel. You are about to cut the end from the tail stock and you need to have a way to drive the pen.

When the end is free, take a light clean-up cut across the end.

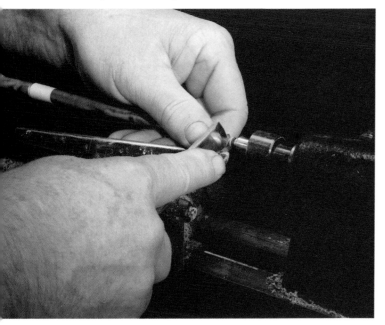

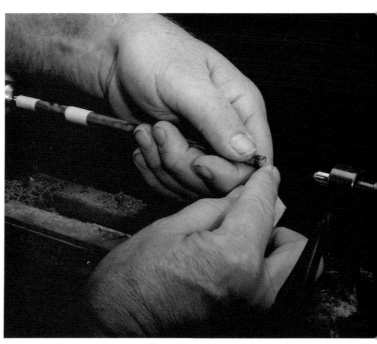

Take successive cuts from each direction with the long point of the skew removing wood to free the pen. Help support everything with your fingers.

Sand the tip and apply French Polish. Make sure you use your fingers to support the piece while you work with the end.

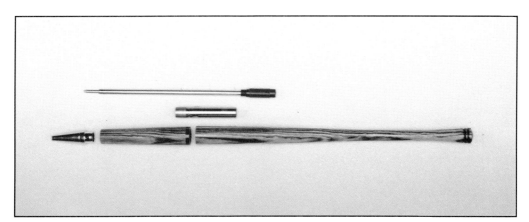

From the kit, you are only using the brass that's already glued into the pen, and the tip, twist mechanism, and the refill shown here with the blanks.

Press in the tip. Then use the vee block to establish the proper depth for the twist mechanism.

TIPS

• I always buy extra brass tubes from the supplier to have a few on hand. Then, if a tube is damaged, I can still complete my project.

• A variable speed hand drill can be used to power the pen mill. Warning: The hand drill is much more aggressive than using the pen mill by hand. The likelihood that you will tear the wood from the brass increases.

• Pen disassembly tools are available through suppliers. They can help take a pen apart without damaging the barrels in case a faulty part interferes with the pen mechanisms or you would like to refinish the pen.

• When drilling oily woods, keep a small wire brush handy to clean the shavings from the drill flutes.

• If you are turning multiple pens, a rack composed of pairs of pins, or dowels to keep each pen's halves together will help you avoid the chaos of mismatched parts.

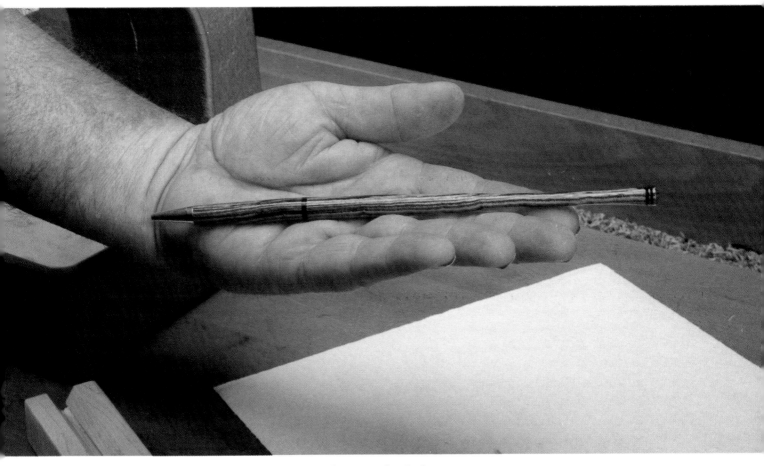

This pen is finished.

A Gallery of Pens

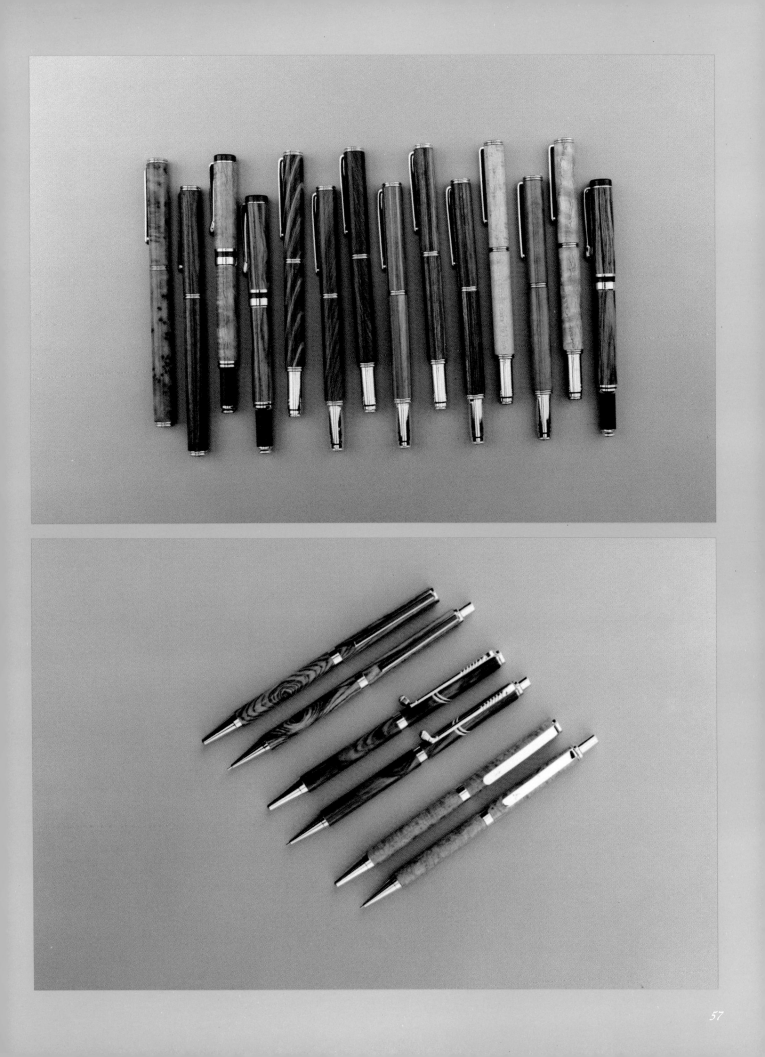

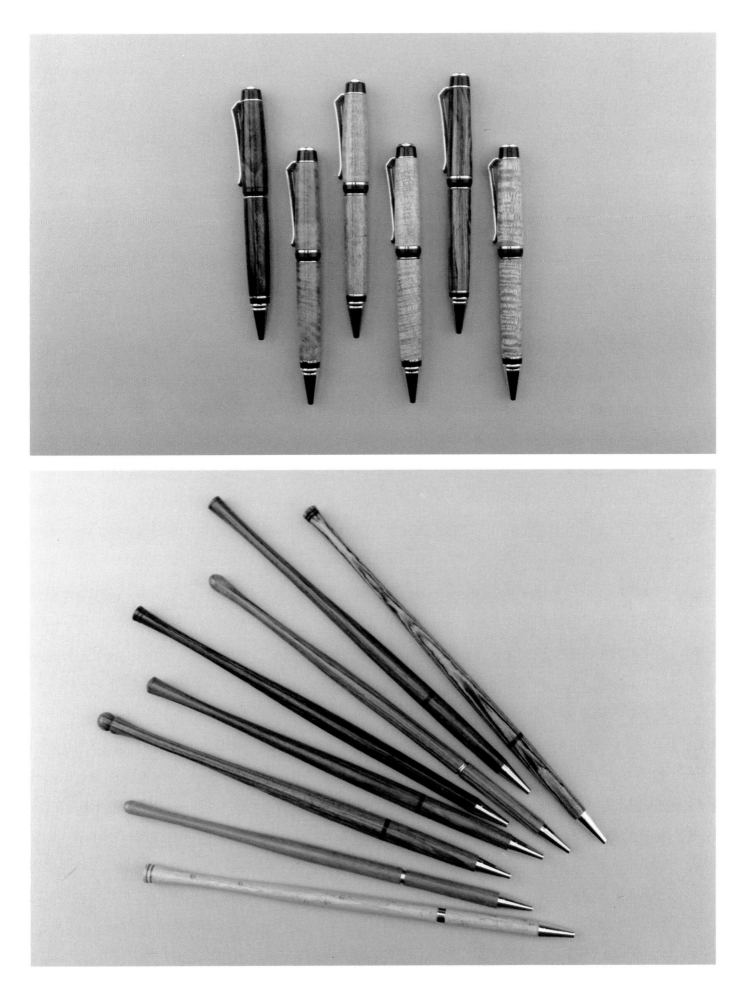

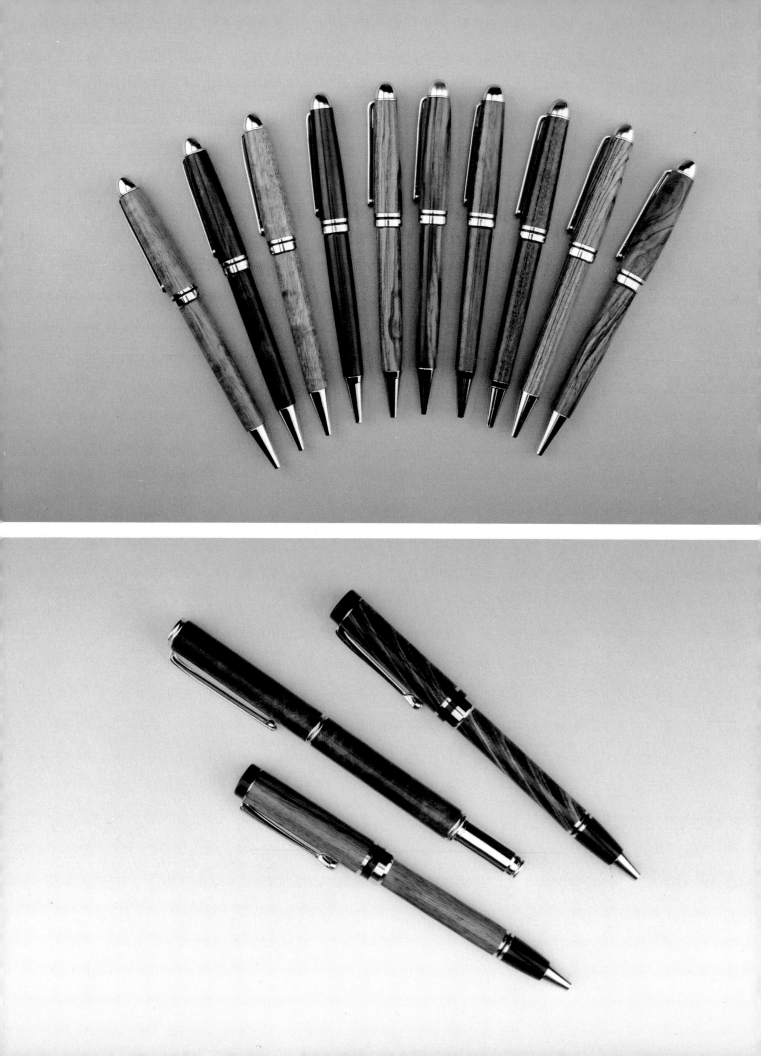

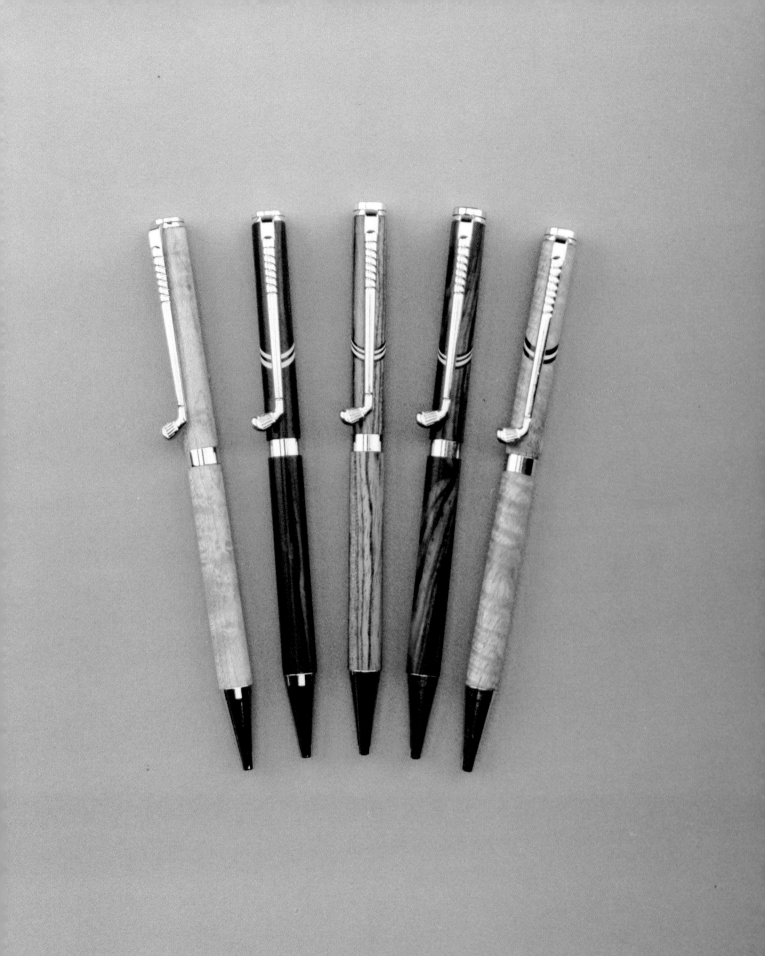

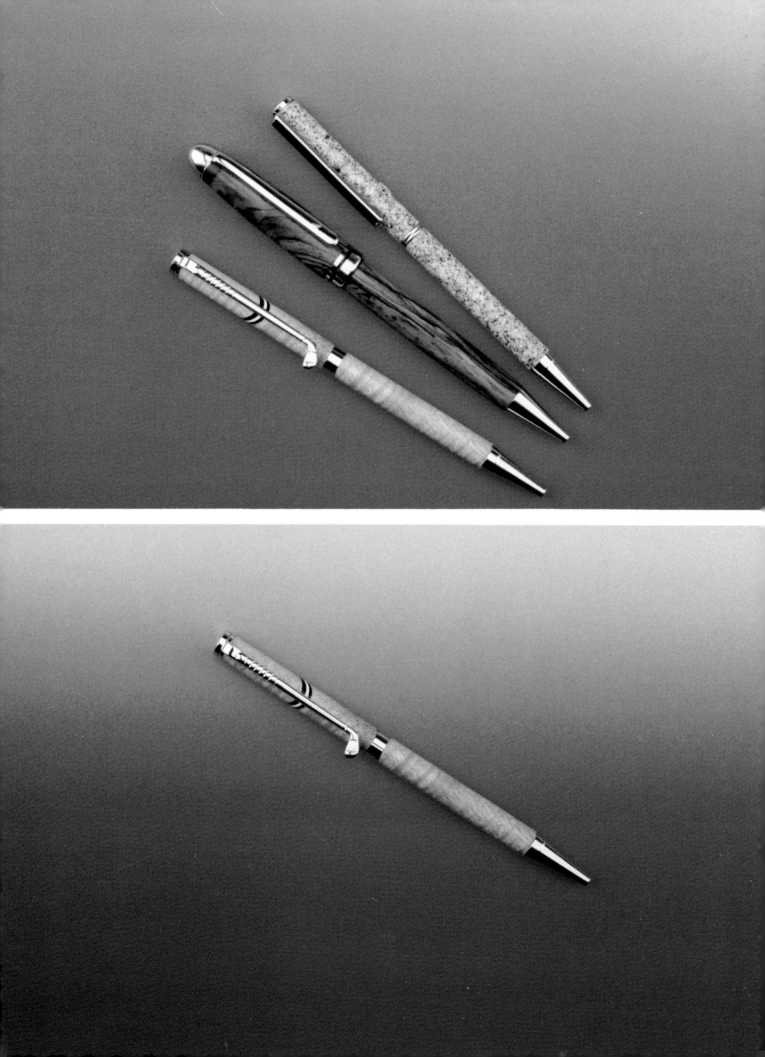

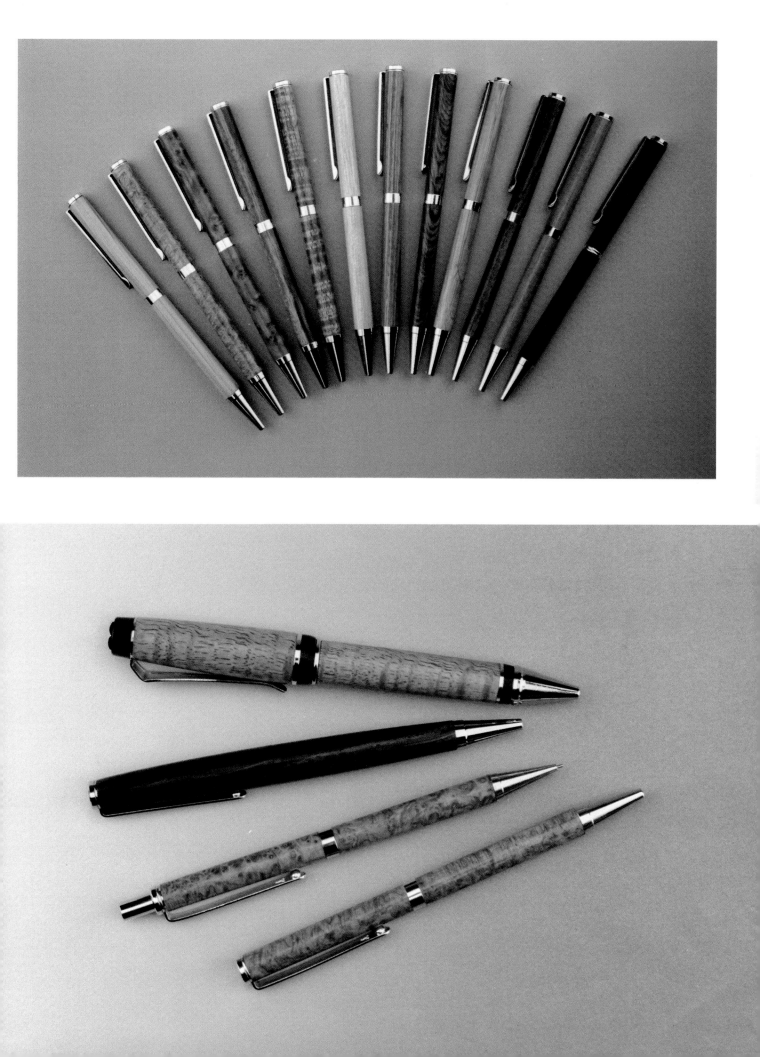